FROM PUERTO RICO, 1937
by Angelo Parra Sr.

From Colombia, 1969
by Patricia Olaya

Two Memoirs About
Newcomers
to the United States

Table of Contents

Memoir

What is a memoir?

A memoir (MEM-wahr) is writing that covers a short period of time in the life of the person writing it. Memoirs focus on the events, thoughts, and feelings of that person. They are often about a specific time or place or a moment in history that is important to the writer. Memoirs communicate the conflict and drama of these events as they unfold, but with a strong personal point of view.

What is the purpose of a memoir?

The purpose of a memoir is to describe events as the writers remember them. These writers want to share their experiences with the rest of the world. Some writers may have lived through important times or contributed to world-changing events. They want readers to know what they did and share what they felt. Writers may also use the memoir as a journey of self-discovery. Writing about the past can help people better understand themselves and how they came to be who they are.

How do you read a memoir?

When you read a memoir, you are reading a first-person narrative: one person's memory of an event or time. Enter into the moment with the writer. Try to picture yourself there. Think about what is important and why the writer chose to write about it. Look for insight into why the event was important to the writer. The writer remembered the moment in great detail. Will you?

A memoir focuses on a short period of time or several related events in a person's life.

A memoir is written in the first person ("I").

A memoir focuses on events the way the author remembers them.

A memoir often includes an ending that makes the reader think.

Features of a Memoir

A memoir includes thoughts and feelings about the events that explain why they are important to the author.

A memoir includes dialogue.

A memoir is written in narrative form and includes story elements such as setting, plot, character development, and conflict.

Who writes memoirs?

In the past, people who took part in world-changing events, like explorations or scientific discoveries, wrote memoirs. The writers wanted to give an eyewitness account of the event. But memoirs are not always about major or public events. You don't have to be famous to write a memoir! People today often write memoirs because a period of time in their lives was important to them. Memoirs can be about everyday events that are interesting to readers because of the way the writer remembers and explains them.

Tools for Readers and Writers

Idiom

Idioms are phrases or expressions that do not use the literal, or exact, meaning of the words. For example, "to catch forty winks" means "to take a nap." Most idioms are inherent to specific cultures and times throughout history. Memoir writers use idioms to give their writing a natural, realistic "you are there" quality, since idioms are very much a part of people's everyday conversation.

Emotion Words

Writers use certain types of words to express joy, anger, fear, and a host of other feelings. These words are called emotion words and are useful in writing that is personal and heartfelt. Since these words convey strong emotions, they reveal the writer's personality and beliefs. Memoir writers are likely to use emotion words because they are being open and honest about themselves.

Author's Purpose

Authors write for different reasons, or purposes, including to entertain, persuade, and inform. Sometimes a book is written with one purpose in mind. Other times, authors write books with many purposes. Memoirs are usually written to provide entertainment and information. But what about the author's purpose for including certain parts of the memoir? These purposes include telling a true story, offering insights into the author's feelings about the events, and describing what the author learned from the events. An author may also have a purpose for organizing their memoir in a certain way. While reading a memoir, ask questions such as *Why did the author include that piece of information?"* or *Will that piece of information help me understand the author's perspective?"*

Newcomers
to the United States

The United States has historically been a country of immigrants—people who come from other places to live here permanently. In the 1600s, the first American settlers came by boat, mostly from Holland and England. They sought religious freedom and economic opportunities.

English settlers at Jamestown

Beginning in the mid-nineteenth century, waves of immigrants from Ireland and Germany came to the United States. From the 1880s to the 1920s, thousands of people, the majority from southern and eastern Europe, arrived on America's shores each year. They were escaping poverty and persecution. European immigration reached a high of over one million people in 1907.

Irish emigrants about to embark on a voyage to the United States

Today, immigrants arrive largely by plane, from all over the world. According to the Office of Immigration Statistics, in 2009 over 743,000 immigrants came to the United States. They came from (in descending order) Asia, other North American countries, Europe, South America, Africa, and other places.

The U.S. continues to attract people seeking the "American Dream." This dream can mean many things: living in freedom, the promise of a good education, a chance for a better life.

Immigrants arriving at Ellis Island in New York City around 1900 (left and below)

A Chinese family in San Francisco's Chinatown, also around 1900

Starting over in a new country is never without challenges. Newcomers leave behind families, friends, and the lives they have always known. They often speak other languages. They must make new friends, start new schools and jobs, and begin a whole new way of life.

As these memoirs show, although it may be a struggle at first, newcomers eventually find their way and become part of the vast "melting pot" that is the United States of America.

These people are taking part in a recent swearing-in ceremony to become U.S. citizens.

FROM PUERTO RICO, 1937

Back in Puerto Rico, we lived across the street from a cathedral, a church that was already old even when I was a boy. The name of the church is Catedral de San Juan Bautista, which is Spanish for the Cathedral of Saint John the Baptist. It was built beginning in 1521, not long after Christopher Columbus arrived from Spain.

But I didn't know any of that in 1937 when I was ten years old. I lived with my father's younger sisters, my aunts Tía Rosa and Tía Manuela, and my brother, Nicolas, who was two years older than me. We lived in San Juan, the biggest city in Puerto Rico, squeezed together in a one-room apartment with cracking walls and peeling paint. There was one bathroom and shower in the building, which all the tenants shared. As bad as this sounds, I thought everybody lived like that.

A city street in San Juan, Puerto Rico (above)
The Cathedral of Saint John the Baptist (right)
Aerial view of San Juan from 1932 (below)

To Nicky and me, the cathedral across the street was just an old building with giant bells that would jolt us out of our sleep on Sunday mornings. People got married in that church, and people had their funerals there.

The only good thing about the Cathedral of Saint John was the baptisms. Nicky and I and our friends would wait outside the big wooden doors when we knew there was a baptism. When the happy family came out of the church, the new godfather would throw a handful of pennies out into the street. We would all scramble in our short pants, pushing and shoving each other, trying to grab up as many pennies as possible. This was a big deal to us, because with two cents a boy could get some candy or buy a small piece of salami from the street vendor. We wished that everyone in Puerto Rico would get baptized, even if they already were.

On hot nights, Tía Rosa and Tía Manuela would sit outside with *las Viejas*, the old ladies of the neighborhood, and tell spooky stories to scare the kids. After we were white-faced and **trembling,** *las Viejas* would laugh and then expect us to go upstairs to our dark rooms alone. There was no electricity in our building back then. People used candles or oil lamps at night.

I didn't know my mother and father. They moved to New York City when I was two years old. There were very few jobs in Puerto Rico, so a lot of Puerto Ricans moved to New York and other cities to get jobs to support their families. Tía Rosa, Tía Manuela, and Nicky were all the family I knew.

In the summer of 1937, I got some exciting and scary news. "*Dentro de poco, iremos a Nueva York,*" Tía Manuela told me and Nicky. My father was sending money to my aunts so that we could move to New York! After so many years, we would be a whole family again with Mamá and Papá!

The trip was to be made by boat. Traveling by airplane was something only wealthy people did. But, as happy as I was to go live in New York, I was **petrified** of the sea trip. What if the boat sank? I didn't know how to swim very well or which direction I would have to swim in to get home. I worried so much I lost weight, and I was skinny to begin with.

Finally, the August day came for Nicky, me, and Tía Manuela to begin our trip. (Tía Rosa wouldn't come to New York for another few years.) Saying good-bye to our San Juan friends and neighbors was hard. But what was most on my mind was the boat.

What would I do if it sank?

I don't remember how many days the boat trip took because I spent the whole voyage sick in my small bed. Seasick. I kept throwing up, over and over, even though I felt too sick to eat anything. So I was relieved when the boat finally arrived and docked on the East Side of Manhattan. I was in New York!

As Tía, Nicky, and I walked off the boat carrying our valises, I saw a friendly-looking, strange man waving to us from behind a fence.

"*Es su papá,*" Tía Manuela whispered to Nicky and me. My father? We waved back excitedly.

Things happened so fast. The next thing I knew, we were riding this noisy, bouncing train that flew through the air between more tall buildings than I had ever seen. We were in an elevated subway train racing uptown. The speed, shaking, and noise scared me. I thought the whole thing would break apart. But Papá and his sister were talking calmly.

"*¿Tienes miedo?*" I asked Nicky. ("Are you scared?")

But I could see he was not scared. Nicky was grinning a grin so big I thought his face would break. So I forced myself to smile, too. With that big phony grin, I must have looked like a chimpanzee.

I was fascinated as the train stopped and started and stopped again, letting hundreds of people— wearing suits and hats and shiny shoes—quickly get on and off.

Through the windows of the subway car, I tried to read the station signs, but I couldn't. Spanish was my language. I didn't know many English words. I realized, for the first time, that in New York City I was going to have to learn a whole new language. I was getting scared again.

When we got to my father's apartment on West 116th Street and Eighth Avenue, I was **spellbound**. The apartment had a kitchen, a bedroom, a living room, electric lights, and its own bathroom. I couldn't believe that only one family would be living in such a huge place!

That night, Nicky and I were told something that made us **downhearted**. Papá and Mamá were divorced. My mother lived someplace else. Our older brother José, now called Joe, lived with her. We would never be a whole family again. Even though I didn't know my mother and father very well, I cried myself to sleep my first night in New York.

In a few weeks, it was time for Nicky and me to start school. When Tía Manuela woke us up

Me on the roof of the apartment building in New York City

that first morning, my father was already out. He and a bunch of his friends had taken two or three trains very early in the morning to get to New Jersey to build new roads. When I grew up, I understood that my father worked for the Works Progress

Administration, or WPA, which was created by President Franklin Roosevelt to make jobs during the Great Depression.

Our new school, P.S. 10, was a few blocks away. Because Nicky was older, he was placed in a higher grade. When, for the first time, I entered the fourth-grade classroom filled with strangers, I felt lonelier than I had ever felt in my life. These kids knew each other and were speaking English a mile a minute. I had no idea what they were saying.

The school day began with the Pledge of Allegiance. When the students stood and faced the flag hanging in the classroom, I stood and faced the flag, too. When all the kids put their right hands on their hearts, so did I. But when they began, "I pledge allegiance to the flag of the United States of America . . . " I had no idea what that meant. I moved my lips, pretending I was reciting whatever it was that the others were reciting. And because everyone was looking at the flag and not at me, I got away with it—for a while. But little by little I learned English by watching and listening to the teacher and my classmates.

Having lived in a warm place, I had never seen snow until that first winter. As this weird and wonderful cold white stuff fell out of the sky, I followed my brother and his friends to nearby Morningside Park. They used sleds and boxes to slide down the snowy hills. I joined in, and it was fun until my feet started to freeze. I was wearing sneakers, and the sneakers were soaked and icing up. Nicky had to carry me home.

One Saturday toward the end of that first school year, when the weather grew warm, Nicky and I visited our mother. This woman, whom we didn't really know, tried to be nice to us. She had married a pleasant man who owned a pharmacy. He had a good business, so Mamá was able to give all of us ten cents each—Nicky, me, and our brother Joe—to go to the movies. For a dime, you could see two black-and-white movies, cartoons, and a newsreel. There was no television at that time.

On one of the first hot summer days in 1938, nearly a year after I moved to the United States, Mamá took the three of us by subway to the beach in Coney Island, Brooklyn. We were used to sunny beaches, but ice cream sodas were new to us. Mamá bought us cold glasses of cola-flavored soda pop with vanilla ice cream

Me on the back of my brother Joe at Coney Island, about a year after I first came to the United States. My other brother, Nicky, is underfoot.

floating on top, and we loved it. To this day, more than seventy years later, on a hot, summer afternoon, an ice cream soda is like a Fountain of Youth for me, and always hits the spot.

But, no matter how much Mamá tried to show us a good time and win our love, she was never that close to

Nicky and me. Perhaps that was because we lived with our father and she had remarried, or maybe it was that she was gone most of the early years of our lives. Looking back, I realize it must have been **devastating** for a young woman to leave her children; no wonder Mamá was always a little distant. Though we came to New York to improve our lives, somewhere along the line, I'm not sure how, we had lost the love of our mother.

Yet, even with the many difficulties that came with moving from Puerto Rico to New York, it was a thrilling time for us. And for me, it was a new beginning.

Angelo Manuel Parra Sr. lived in San Juan, Puerto Rico, until he was ten when he moved to New York City. For a while, he was a member of the Boy Scouts. When he got older, he studied business at Central Commercial High School in Manhattan. At age eighteen, Angelo was drafted into the U.S. Army. He spent a year of his military service in Japan. After his discharge, he married Edith Ruiz.

For a few years, Angelo worked in a pharmacy. In 1953, he went to work for a company that made metal parts used by dentists to repair teeth.

In 1964, Angelo and Edith, with their three sons—Angelo Jr., Larry, and Billy—moved from city housing projects into a house in the Bronx. Angelo became a member of the Lions Club, a community service organization, and served as the club's president for a year.

Today, Angelo Parra Sr. is retired. He and Edith still live in the house in the Bronx.

Analyze the Memoir

- Whom is the memoir about?
- What is the memoir about?
- What other people are involved in the memoir?
- This memoir includes thoughts the author had while the events were taking place. Identify two.
- This memoir includes thoughts the author has right now about what happened in the past. Identify two.
- What did the author learn from writing his memoir?
- How does the memoir end?

Focus on Comprehension: Author's Purpose

- On page 8, the author says that his family was "squeezed together in a one-room apartment." Why does the author use those words to describe his home?
- On page 13 of the memoir, the author includes an event concerning the Pledge of Allegiance. Why does the author include this event?
- For what purpose does the author include the photographs in his memoir?

Analyze the Tools Writers Use: Idiom

- On page 11, the author says, "I thought his face would break." What does the author mean by this expression?
- On page 13, the author says that the kids in school were "speaking English a mile a minute." How can the English language move? How is this phrase an idiom?
- On page 14, the author says that an ice cream soda always "hits the spot." This idiom means that ice cream on a very hot day is a good thing. What evidence from the text supports the idiom's meaning?

Focus on Words: Emotion Words

Make a chart like the one below. Locate each word in the memoir. Read the sentences around the word and determine a possible definition using context clues and the dictionary. Finally, decide what the emotion word adds to the memoir.

Page	Word	Dictionary definition	What does the emotion word add to the memoir?
10	trembling		
10	petrified		
12	spellbound		
12	downhearted		
15	devastating		

From Colombia, 1969

As I ride the Number Seven subway to my office on the fifty-third floor of a glass skyscraper in midtown Manhattan or walk up Madison Avenue where I buy a bagel and coffee from a street vendor, I feel like New York City has always been my home. My English, after all, is close to perfect; I doubt that anyone but a linguist could detect an accent. Only a few of my friends can tell that I'm from somewhere else: the city of Cali, in the country of Colombia in South America. I'm actually quite proud of how "American" I have become, given that I came to the United States when I was already eight years old. Back then, in October 1969, I spoke just a few words of English. I was a stranger in a strange place.

The San Antonio district, where I come from, is one of the oldest parts of Cali. I grew up on a street with 200-year-old adobe homes. I lived with my parents and my brother, Fabian, two years younger than me. I remember that when I looked up from my bedroom window, I could see a big white cathedral.

We lived in a neighborhood with loads of kids. We had a very large extended family living near us. My grandparents lived directly across the street. Aunt Mildred, my mom's older sister, lived right down the block. In all, there were more than twenty first cousins right in the neighborhood! My birthday parties were so large the crowd would spill into the street. Life was great and then I turned eight. . . .

It was January 2, 1969, and my parents gave me the biggest birthday bash ever. My dad rearranged the living room furniture so we could fit many folding tables and chairs in it for the celebration. My mom was up early that day making my favorite dish, chicken and rice. She also made a huge fruit torte.

I don't remember every detail of that day as it was more than forty years ago. What I do remember is that the crowd sang "Happy Birthday" to me in Spanish ("*Feliz Cumpleaños*"). My grandmother helped me blow out all the candles because I was so **flustered** by all the attention paid to me. But when I saw that my grandmother had tears in her eyes, I couldn't understand why.

The memoir focuses on events the way the author remembers them.

I asked her, *"Abuela, ¿por qué tan triste?"* ("Grandma, why are you so sad?") This was a happy occasion. She said that we would talk about it later.

Trying to forget her **mournful** expression, I opened a stack of presents in colorful wrappings that were piled high on the piano. Once the guests had left, my grandmother hugged me and said that this was probably the last time that she would ever be at one of my birthday parties. Tears filled her eyes. I ran to the kitchen and **confronted** my parents. I asked them why would this be the last party that my grandmother would be at. Was she sick? Then my dad told me that we were leaving Colombia for "new opportunities" in the United States. I stood there in my yellow party dress, frozen in time, unable to hear what he was saying. It seemed that my dad was being transferred to New York by his company. My dad thought it would be a great career opportunity and a fabulous experience for my brother and me.

That night, and for many more, I begged and **implored** my parents to change their plans and to stay right where we were. I did not want to leave my grandparents, my cousins, my friends, or my school. I did not need new opportunities; my life was just fine! Now I can almost laugh at how I carried on. But boy, was I miserable then!

The memoir includes thoughts and feelings about the events that explain why they are important to the author. By writing about the past, she gets some new insights into herself.

20

My dad left soon thereafter to try out his new job, find us an apartment, and get settled. He wrote us letters saying that he found a nice apartment in Elmhurst, Queens, in New York City and that he loved the energy of this new place. My mother read the letters aloud to my brother and me, hoping that we would get excited by this new adventure.

I missed my father but was still angry at him for making us move. My mother was getting us packed up for our new lives in the United States. She said that I could take my favorite doll, Carolina, but not her doll furniture as it was too big to pack. She promised to replace it when we got to New York. I was devastated when she sold

This photo was taken the day my father left for the United States.

it at a tag sale along with our bookcases, dining table, and pots and pans. This was our lives. That's when it hit me: Who will I play with? Who will I talk to in this new place? It didn't help that my older cousin told me that the people in America were giants and that I better watch my step or I could be crushed under their feet.

The memoir includes dialogue as it is remembered and recreated by the author.

Another cousin said that New York City was a place *"muy peligroso"* ("very dangerous") because kids were snatched away from their parents all the time.

I was terrified when we arrived at the airport on that October day in 1969 with a one-way ticket to New York City. Friends and family members came to the airport to wish us well. My grandmother gave me a lavender orchid on a bracelet that I later pressed into my diary. I hugged and kissed her with all my heart and never wanted to let her go. I still have that orchid and I take it out and look at it when I want to think about my grandmother or a family event.

I don't remember much about the flight to New York, but I do remember the sign that read "International Arrivals" at JFK airport and hearing my brother scream, "PAPÁ!" He waved wildly at my father standing behind a huge glass window. Once we passed through customs, Papá was there with open arms to embrace the three of us. As I took his hand, never wanting to let it go, I could see that he, too, had been crying.

The author of the memoir includes emotional moments.

We walked through the airport and I remember looking for the giants. I did not see any; rather, people were the same size as back home. My cousin had pulled a fast one! But English was what I heard spoken everywhere, along with snatches of other unfamiliar languages. This both thrilled and frightened me.

My father loaded up our luggage in the 1958 gun-metal gray Rambler station wagon that he had bought for us. We arrived at our new home: a seven-story, brick apartment building; Apartment 1L on the ground floor was ours. It was a two-bedroom apartment so my brother and I had to share a room. It was late at night. We went right to sleep.

The memoir includes story elements such as setting. Here, the author includes details about her family car and new home.

The next morning, from our bedroom window, we saw the street in front of our apartment filled with kids riding bicycles, drawing with sidewalk chalk, and jumping rope. Excited to join them, my brother and I quickly ran out. No one spoke Spanish so at first my brother and I stuck together, feeling like Martians. Then I saw two girls in matching green belted dresses with bandannas around their necks and wondered why they were wearing uniforms on a Sunday. It turned out that the older of the two knew a few words of Spanish. She asked, "*¿Cómo te llamas?*" ("What is your name?") I realize now that they were wearing their Girl Scout uniforms!

The Olaya family, about a year after we moved to the United States

Her name was Amalia and she told me that she was one of four sisters who lived in the apartment next to ours, in apartment 1M. Her family was also from Colombia, from the capital city of Bogotá. Her parents had moved to New York ten years ago. Not only did Amalia and I become fast friends, but our families did, too. I also met Sasha, a girl my age from a Russian family who lived on the second floor, and Marie, from the top floor, a year older than me, who had recently moved from Jamaica. Things were starting to look up for me and my "foreign" friends. Meanwhile, my brother Fabian, who was only seven, immediately found friends to play soccer with. He never again mentioned his old life in Colombia and if he missed it, he never let us know. I should ask him sometime what was going through his mind.

My new school was P.S. 89 in Elmhurst, Queens, an old brick building surrounded by a tall, chain-link fence. Since I knew very little English, the principal told my mother and me, through a translator, that I was to be placed in the first grade even though I was eight years old and a **legitimate** third grader! I held back the tears when I heard this but tried to tough it out. Fortunately, the plan didn't work very well as my mother knew my daily "stomach aches" were really because I was bored with the baby work and wanted to be with kids my own age.

The author introduces the characters that are important to this section of the memoir: the kids in her new neighborhood.

Elementary schoolchildren
in Queens, 1968

I changed classes and that made a huge difference. As soon as I walked into Mrs. O'Leary's third-grade class, I knew things were going to work out. There I met Yola Tumos, a girl from Yugoslavia, and Heidi Livadariu, a girl from Romania. None of us spoke English very well but we became friends. Two months later the three of us were completely fluent in English. That was quite an accomplishment!

On January 2, 1970, when I turned nine, my two new friends came over to celebrate. My parents were amazed as the three of us spoke only in English! It was a very happy birthday.

A memoir often includes an ending that makes the reader think.

Postscript

Was my dad correct when he said moving to the United States would be a fabulous experience? Well, I am fluent in two languages, and I got an excellent education. I've met people from many countries and cultures. What's more, I've learned there are kind, friendly, and interesting people everywhere. Most people will accept you when you are a newcomer; you just have to give them a chance.

He definitely made the right choice moving to Queens. This borough of New York City is a true melting pot. Immigrants from all over the world have been settling in Queens for the past hundred years and there is no sign of this slowing down. More languages are spoken in Queens than in any area of the United States! On a single street you can get excellent Chinese, Korean, and Latin American food, not to mention a real bagel. Plus, it is only a subway ride to Manhattan.

Patricia Olaya earned a degree in Spanish literature and biochemistry from Saint John's University and worked as a paralegal, then as an investment assistant for an insurance company. She went on to get a master's degree in international finance. She is now a senior vice president and trust officer for TIAA-CREF. She still lives in Queens, New York.

Analyze the Memoir

- Whom is the memoir about?
- What is the memoir about?
- What other people are involved in the memoir?
- This memoir includes thoughts the author had while the events were taking place. Identify two.
- This memoir includes thoughts the author has right now about what happened in the past. Identify two.
- What did the author learn from writing her memoir?
- How does the memoir end?

Focus on Comprehension: Author's Purpose

- On page 19, the author says that she had "more than twenty first cousins right in the neighborhood." Why do you think the author thought this information was important to include in her memoir?
- On page 25, the author tells about meeting Amalia. Why does the author include this event?
- On page 25, the author tells readers that a translator was needed on her first day of school. For what purpose does the author include this piece of information?

Focus on Including Foreign Languages

When people immigrate to the United States, they bring their languages with them. When immigrants write their memoirs, they often include bits and pieces of their native language to make the memoirs more personal to them and more interesting to the reader. Both memoirs in this book contains sentences spoken in Spanish. Locate them in the memoirs. Ask yourself, "How do these sentences enhance the memoirs? How does the use of the Spanish language make me feel about the memoirs?"

Analyze the Tools Writers Use: Idiom

- On page 23, the author says, "My cousin had pulled a fast one!" What does the author mean by this idiom?
- On page 25, the author says that she and Amalia became "fast friends." This idiom means that they became very good friends. What evidence from the text supports the idiom's meaning?
- On page 25, the author says, "Things were starting to look up for me." How can things look up? How is this phrase an idiom?

Focus on Words: Emotion Words

Make a chart like the one below. Locate each word in the memoir. Read the sentences around the word and determine a possible definition using context clues and the dictionary. Finally, decide what the emotion word adds to the memoir.

Page	Word	Dictionary definition	What does the emotion word add to the memoir?
19	flustered		
20	mournful		
20	confronted		
20	implored		
25	legitimate		

How does an author write a

Memoir?

Reread "From Colombia, 1969" and think about what Patricia Olaya did to write this memoir. How does she show how important this event was in her life? How does she make you feel as if you were there?

❶ Decide on an important event or period in your life.

Remember that a memoir is an actual retelling of something you have experienced. It allows you to relive that time and reflect upon the emotions you feel now as a type of "self-discovery." In "From Colombia, 1969," the author shares memories of her family's move from South America to the United States. She expresses both how she reacted to this life-changing event as an eight-year-old girl and how she feels about it today.

❷ Decide who else should be in your memoir.

Other people often play a large part in the important events of your life. Ask yourself:

- Who was with me?
- Which people had the most impact on my experience?
- How will I describe these people?
- How did these people feel about the event?
- Did these people add to the conflict or help overcome it?

Person	Impact on author's experience
grandmother	sorrowful that family was moving away
parents	tried to instill excitement about the family's new adventure
cousin	tried to frighten author about what might happen
brother	showed how easy it is to make new friends
Amalia	first new friend in the United States
Mrs. O'Leary	helped author learn to speak English
Yola and Heidi	helped celebrate first birthday in new home

❸ Recall setting and events.

Jot down notes about what happened and where it happened. Ask yourself:

- Where did the important events take place? How will I describe these places?
- What was the situation or problem I experienced? Was the experience happy, scary, sad, or surprising?
- What parts do I remember most? Why are these incidents memorable?
- How did my experience turn out?
- What questions might my readers have that I could answer in my memoir?
- What did I learn about myself from this experience? What more did I learn by writing about it?

Element of memoir	Details	Effect on author
Settings	Neighborhood in Cali, Colombia, South America and neighborhood of Elmhurst, Queens, in New York City	She loved having grandparents across the street and more than twenty first cousins nearby. "Life was great and then I turned eight. . . ."
Situation or problem	had to leave home, relatives, friends, and school behind when family moved to the United States	She was devastated, begged parents to change their plans, did not want new opportunities, thought life was just fine as it was.
Events	1. Patricia had her eighth birthday party in Colombia. 2. She found out her family was moving. 3. Father left to prepare for family. 4. The family flew to New York. 5. Patricia made new friends in neighborhood. 6. She started school—made more new friends and learned to speak fluent English. 7. She had her ninth birthday party in the United States.	She will always remember the biggest birthday bash ever, couldn't understand why they had to move, was angry at father, devastated to sell belongings they couldn't take, worried about dangers and who she would play with, joyful to reunite with father, thrilled and frightened to hear new language, excited to join other children playing outside but felt "like Martians" until she made new friends, was upset to start school until she moved to Mrs. O'Leary's class, was proud to speak English with new friends at ninth birthday party.
How my experience turned out	She still lives and works in New York City.	She made peace with the move; NYC now feels like home.

Glossary

confronted   (kun-FRUN-ted) caused a challenge; faced head-on (page 20)

devastating   (DEH-vuh-stay-ting) bringing ruin or an overwhelming sense of helplessness (page 15)

downhearted   (down-HAR-ted) low or sad in spirits; dejected (page 12)

flustered   (FLUS-terd) made to behave in a confused, self-conscious way (page 19)

implored   (im-PLORD) asked with great urgency and anguish; begged (page 20)

legitimate   (lih-JIH-tih-mut) by rights; in accordance with law or custom (page 25)

mournful   (MORN-ful) full of sadness and gloom (page 20)

petrified   (PEH-trih-fide) frozen with fear (page 10)

spellbound   (SPEL-bownd) as if held in the power of a magic spell; entranced (page 12)

trembling   (TREM-bling) shaking with fear (page 10)